Little Scientists

Discover the world of science through
fun and challenging experiments for
young explorers

Author: Chris Winder

Dear young explorers of science,

Welcome to this extraordinary journey through the world of learning, imagination and invention! This book is your personal passport to adventure, exploration and discovery of what makes our world so amazingly fascinating.

Remember, however, that every great adventure requires prudence and responsibility. As you dive into the pages of this book and try to carry out our exciting experiments, it is very important that you always ask permission and the presence of an adult. Not only for your safety, but also to share the joy of discovery with those you love.

Science experiments are a fantastic way to learn, but as with any journey into the unknown, it's crucial to have an expert guide by your side. An adult can help you understand instructions, handle tools safely, and answer your questions.

Never forget that safety is the number one priority! Some of the experiments in this book may require the use of materials or tools that, if not handled correctly, could be dangerous. Don't let your excitement lead you to forget these important precautions.

Now, get ready to enter the wonderful world of science! From chemists to physicists, biologists to astronomers, you'll find yourself wearing many different hats throughout these adventures. And remember, every great scientist started somewhere, just like you.

Get ready to discover, learn and above all have fun! Are you ready? So, ask permission, make sure you have an adult by your side, put your safety first and start your scientific adventure!

With enthusiasm,

The FRGG NEW PRESS BOOKS Team

Chapter 1: Water Experiments

Hi guys! Welcome to our first chapter, where we will delve into the mysterious and wonderful world of water. Water is everywhere around us – in lakes, rivers, oceans and even within us! But do you know what water really is and what it can do? Are you ready to discover some surprising secrets? So, let's get to work!

Remember: for every experiment, you will need an adult by your side. Before starting, ask permission and prepare all the necessary materials together.

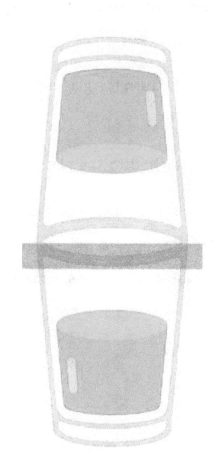

Experiment 1: Water That Doesn't Fall

For this experiment you will need a full glass of water, a piece of cardboard and a little courage.

Fill the glass with water to the brim.

Place the piece of cardboard over the glass, completely covering the opening.

Holding the cardboard in place, quickly turn the glass upside down.

Surprise! The cardboard remains attached to the glass and the water does not fall off.

This experiment shows you how the air around us puts pressure on everything, even the water in the glass, holding the cardboard in place.

Experiment 2: The Rainbow in Water

For this experiment you will need a glass of water, a sheet of white paper and a sunny day.

Fill the glass with water almost to the brim.

Place the glass near the window where sunlight can hit the water directly.

Place the sheet of white paper on the floor or on a nearby table, so that the light passing through the water in the glass falls on the sheet.

Observe how the light separates into different colors, creating a small rainbow on the paper.

This experiment shows you how water can function as a prism, separating white light into its different colored components.

Guys, we just scratched the surface of the immense expanse of water of science. There are still so many fantastic experiments to do and discover. Always remember, safety first and have fun in your scientific adventure!

1.1 Water Surface Experiment

Ready for another exciting experiment? This time, we will see an incredible property of water called surface tension.

You will need a glass of water, some black pepper and some dishwashing liquid.

Fill the glass with water almost to the brim.

Sprinkle a little black pepper on the surface of the water. You will see that the pepper floats!

Now, dip a finger in dishwashing liquid, then gently touch the surface of the water in the glass.

Surprise! Pepper quickly moves to the edges of the glass.

What happened? Water has a kind of "skin" on its surface, called surface tension. When you added the detergent, you stopped this surface tension and the pepper was quickly pushed towards the edges of the glass.

1.2 Water Density Experiment

Now, we will learn something fascinating about water density. You will need a large glass, a small glass, water, olive oil and corn syrup.

Fill the large glass half with water.

Fill the small glass half with olive oil and the other half with corn syrup.

Slowly pour the contents of the small glass into the large glass.

Watch what happens: olive oil floats on water, while corn syrup sinks.

This experiment demonstrates the density of liquids. Corn syrup is thicker than water, so it sinks, while olive oil is less thick than water, so it floats.

Remember, guys, safety is always the number one priority! Always ask for permission and the presence of an adult when doing these experiments. And remember, science is also fun, so enjoy every experiment!

1.3 Water Capillarity Experiment

Now, we're going to delve into a fascinating phenomenon called capillarity. This is the process that allows water to rise against the force of gravity! You will need a glass of water, two pieces of absorbent paper and two food dyes of different colors.

Half fill the glass with water.

Add a few drops of a food coloring on one side of the glass and a few drops of the other dye on the other side.

Take the two pieces of absorbent paper and fold them in half along the length. These represent our "capillaries".

Place one end of each strip of paper towels in the water cup and the other end out of the glass, making sure the two pieces of paper do not touch.

See what happens. You will see the colors rise along the strips of paper and, eventually, they will begin to mix where they meet outside the glass.

This is an example of capillarity, the process that allows water (and the food dyes in it) to rise against gravity through the capillaries of paper. It is the same principle that allows plants to absorb water from the soil through their roots!

Remember, guys, science is everywhere around us, even in the simplest things like a glass of water. And while you're having fun with these experiments, always remember to put safety first and have an adult with you.

Chapter 2: Nature Experiments

Hi guys! Are you ready for another scientific adventure? This time, we will leave the laboratory and enter the largest classroom of all: nature! Here, we will discover how plants grow, how animals behave and how all the elements of nature work together in perfect harmony.

As always, remember: for every experiment, you will need an adult by your side. Before starting, ask permission and prepare all the necessary materials together.

Experiment 1: Growing a Bean in a Jar

For this experiment you will need a glass jar, a bean, cotton and water.

Wet the cotton with water and put it in the jar.

Place the bean between the cotton and the side of the jar so you can see it.

Observe the bean every day and add water if necessary.

After a while, you will see the bean sprout and begin to grow. This experiment shows you how plants grow and how they need water to live.

Experiment 2: Creating an Insect Habitat

For this experiment you will need a plastic jar with a lid, earth, leaves, sticks and, of course, some insect such as an ant or ladybug.

Half fill the jar with soil.

Add leaves and sticks to create an environment similar to that in which insects live.

Finally, gently add the insect to the jar.

Remember, this is only a temporary habitat! After observing the insect for a while, be sure to release it where you found it.

These experiments will help you better understand how nature works. Always remember to respect all life forms and handle with care any creature you come across.

Remember, guys, safety is always the number one priority! Always ask for permission and the presence of an adult when doing these experiments. And remember, science is also fun, so enjoy every experiment!

2.1 Photosynthesis experiment

Hi guys! Today we will delve into the magical process called photosynthesis. This is how plants produce their food, and we'll play the role of little plant detectives to find out how it works. You will need a plant, a transparent plastic bag and a rubber band.

Choose an outdoor plant that gets plenty of sunlight during the day.

Take a branch with some healthy leaves and cover it with the plastic bag, making sure that it is tightly sealed with the elastic.

Leave the plant in the sun for a day.

When you return the next day, you should see small drops of water inside the bag. These drops are the product of photosynthesis. During this process, the plant takes water from the soil and carbon dioxide from the air, and with the energy of the sun produces oxygen (which is released into the air) and glucose (the food for the plant). Excess water is released through the pores of the leaves, a process called perspiration, which you can see in the form of water droplets in the bag.

Isn't that fascinating? Plants are real food factories, and all they need is water, air and sunlight!

As always, remember to do these experiments under adult supervision and treat all living creatures, including trees and plants, with respect and care.

2.2 Seed Germination Experiment

Hello science adventurers! Today we will take an exciting journey into the world of seed germination. This is the process in which a seed begins to develop a new plant. For this experiment, you'll need some seeds (such as beans, peas, or lentils), a clear container (such as a glass jar or clear plastic bag), cotton, and water.

Wet the cotton with water but without drowning it. It should be damp, but not completely submerged.

Put the damp cotton in the transparent container.

Place some seeds on top of the damp cotton.

Place the container in a warm place, but not directed to sunlight.

Observe the seeds daily, making sure the cotton stays moist.

After a few days, you should start to see seeds opening and small green shoots sprouting up. These shoots are the beginning of a new plant! The seedling is using the food reserves stored in the seed to grow until it can photosynthesize on its own.

Remember, guys, science is everywhere around us, even in a small seed. And while you're having fun with these experiments, always remember to put safety first and have an adult with you.

2.3 Air Pollution Experiment

Hello, young explorers! Today we are going to address a very important problem: air pollution. We will see how we can detect the presence of polluting particles in the air we breathe. For this experiment, you will need a piece of white paper, petroleum jelly and duct tape.

Spread a layer of Vaseline on one side of the white piece of paper. Make sure that the entire surface is covered.

Apply adhesive tape on the edges of the paper, leaving the part with Vaseline uncovered.

Find an outdoor place where you can stick your card, such as a wall or pole. Make sure it's a place where the card can stay for a few days without being disturbed.

Leave the card there for at least 3-4 days.

After this period, look at the card. If you see dark spots or dust on Vaseline, they are polluting particles that were in the air!

This experiment shows how air pollution is not always visible, but it can be detected. Remember, each of us has a role to play in protecting our planet and reducing pollution.

We can do our part by using the car less, recycling and reducing waste.

Remember, guys, safety is always the number one priority! Always ask for permission and the presence of an adult when doing these experiments. And remember, science is also fun, so enjoy every experiment!

Chapter 3: Experiments on Light

Hello, young scientists! Today we will delve into the bright and fascinating world of light. We will see how it reflects, refracts and changes when it passes through different materials. And remember, for every experiment, you'll need an adult by your side. Before starting, ask permission and prepare all the necessary materials together.

Experiment 1: Light Reflection

For this experiment you will need a flashlight, a mirror and a dark room.

Turn on the flashlight and point it at the mirror.

Observe how the light reflects off the mirror and illuminates another part of the room.

This is an example of light reflection. Light travels in a straight line until it encounters an object, such as the mirror, which reflects it in a new direction.

Experiment 2: Refraction of Light

For this experiment you will need a glass of water and a pencil.

Fill the glass with water.

Put the pencil in the glass.

Look at the pencil through the side of the glass. It looks broken or tilted, doesn't it?

This is an example of light refraction. When light passes from one material to another (in this case, from air to water), it changes speed, which makes it seem like the object breaks or tilts.

Experiment 3: Light scattering

For this experiment you will need a prism or a CD and a light source.

Point the light source at the prism or CD.

Observe how the light divides into various colors.

This is an example of light scattering. When white light passes through a prism or reflects off a CD, it splits into the colors of the rainbow.

Remember, guys, safety is always the number one priority! Always ask for permission and the presence of an adult when doing these experiments. And remember, science is also fun, so enjoy every experiment!

3.1 Light Reflection Experiment

Hello, young explorers of light! Today we will do an experiment that will make you look like magicians: we will "blow" the light! This phenomenon is called light reflection, and all you will need is a flashlight, a mirror and a white wall.

Go to a room that you can make quite dark by closing the curtains or shutters.

Turn on the flashlight and point it at the mirror. Hold the mirror so that it is slightly tilted relative to the flashlight.

Slowly move the mirror until you see a spot of light reflecting off the white wall.

You feel like magic, right? In fact, it's pure science! This is an example of light reflection. Light travels in a straight line and when it encounters a reflective surface, like a mirror, it bounces off it, just like a ball bounces off a wall. That's why you see the point of light on the wall!

Remember, safety first! Make sure you have an adult with you while you do this experiment and never point direct light into someone's eyes.

Until next time.

3.2 Light Refraction Experiment

Hello, little scientists of light! Today we will have fun with an experiment that will make you see things differently. We are talking about the refraction of light, a phenomenon that occurs when light changes speed passing from one material to another. You will need a glass of water, a pencil and an endless curiosity!

Fill the glass with water to the brim.

Take the pencil and put it in the glass, making sure that part of the pencil is still out of the water.

Look at the pencil through the side of the glass. Does this sound strange?

The pencil looks broken or tilted, doesn't it? This is because of the refraction of light! When light passes from air to water, it changes speed, and this makes it seem like the pencil bends. Isn't that fascinating?

Remember, guys, safety is always the number one priority! Always ask for permission and the presence of an adult when doing these experiments. And best of all, have fun while you learn!

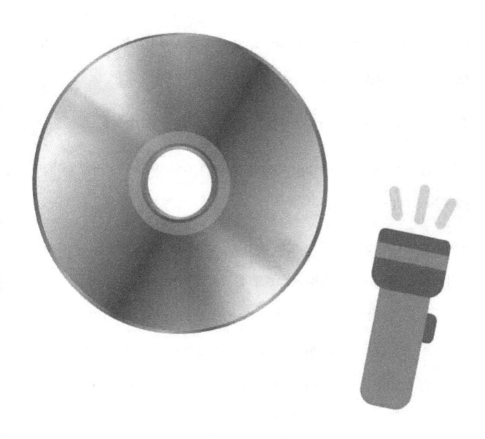

3.3 Color Separation Experiment

Hello, young color detectives! Today we will have fun with an experiment that will turn white light into a rainbow of colors. This phenomenon is called light scattering, and for this experiment you will need a prism (or CD) and a torch.

Go to a room that you can make quite dark by closing the curtains or shutters.

Turn on the flashlight and point it at the prism or CD.

Observe how white light splits into many different colors, just like a rainbow.

Here's what's happening: white light is made up of many different colors. When it passes through the prism or reflects on the CD, each color changes speed slightly differently and this causes color separation. This is the same principle that creates rainbows in the sky after rain!

Remember, guys, safety is always the number one priority! Always ask for permission and the presence of an adult when doing these experiments. And above all, have fun while discovering the secrets of light!

Until next time.

Chapter 4: Chemical Experiments

Hello, budding young chemists! Are you ready to explore the exciting and mysterious world of chemistry? In this chapter, we will do experiments that will show you how certain substances react with each other in surprising ways. And remember, for every experiment, you'll need an adult by your side. Before starting, ask permission and prepare all the necessary materials together.

Experiment 1: Eruption of a Home Volcano

Have you ever wanted to see a volcanic eruption up close? Well, with this experiment, you can do it safely. You will need a glass, vinegar, baking soda and red food coloring.

Experiment 2: Hopping Eggs

This experiment will show you how chemistry can make a raw egg rubbery and bouncy. You will need an egg, a glass and vinegar.

Material needed:

Raw egg

Glass or jar large enough to hold the egg completely submerged

White vinegar

Gloves and safety glasses (optional but recommended)

Procedure:

Wear gloves and safety glasses to ensure safe handling during the experiment.

Gently place the raw egg in the glass or jar. Be careful not to break it.

Pour the vinegar into the glass until the egg is completely covered. You will see small bubbles begin to form on the egg, a sign that the vinegar is starting to react with the shell of the egg.

Leave the egg in vinegar for at least 24 hours. During this time, the vinegar will slowly dissolve the shell of the egg.

After 24 hours, carefully remove the egg from the glass. Only the inner lining of the egg should be left, which is rubbery and flexible. Rinse the egg under running water to remove any shell residue.

Now you have a "hopping egg". It is rubbery and can bounce from a small height. However, be careful because if it falls from too high a height, the egg will break.

Explanation:

This experiment is a fun way to observe a chemical reaction. Vinegar, which is an acid, reacts with calcium carbonate in the shell of the egg. This reaction produces carbon dioxide gas, which you see as bubbles during the experiment. This process will dissolve the shell of the egg, leaving only the inner membrane which is rubbery and flexible.

When bounced, the egg demonstrates the elastic properties of the inner membrane. However, the membrane is not strong enough to withstand a fall from a high height, so the egg will break if it falls from too high. Remember, it's still a raw egg inside!

Always remember to do scientific experiments in a safe environment and, if possible, under adult supervision. Have fun with science!

Experiment 3: DIY Crystals

Who wouldn't like to grow their own crystals at home? With this experiment, you can do it! You will need water, salt, a glass jar and a little patience.

Remember, guys, safety is always the number one priority! Chemistry can be a lot of fun, but it's important to follow the instructions and always have an adult present. And remember, science is also fun, so enjoy every experiment!

Until next time.

4.1 Experiment with Baking Soda and Vinegar

Hello, young chemists! Ready to create some chemical magic? Today we will do an experiment that will look like a volcanic explosion, all with materials you already have at home! You'll need baking soda, vinegar, a glass or jar, and to make things a little more spectacular, red food coloring.

Start by placing a couple of tablespoons of baking soda in the glass or jar.

Add a few drops of red food coloring.

Now it's time for the eruption! Pour a little vinegar into the glass.

Boom! You have just created your own mini-volcanic eruption! But what happened? Baking soda (a base) and vinegar (an acid) reacted together to form a gas called carbon dioxide. This gas has created all those effervescent bubbles that have made your volcano "erupt".

Remember, safety first! Make sure you have an adult with you while you do this experiment, and since it might make a bit of a mess, you might want to do it outdoors or on an easy-to-clean surface.

Until next time

4.2 Experiment with Lemon and Bicarbonate

Hello, little scientists! Are you ready for another adventurous chemical experiment? Today we will create a small lemon volcano right in our house! You will need a lemon, baking soda, a teaspoon, and for an extra effect, red food coloring.

Take a lemon and cut it in half. An adult should make this step.

Use the teaspoon to dig a little 'lemon pulp, creating a small bowl.

Add a teaspoon of baking soda to the lemon bowl you just created.

For a touch of drama, add a few drops of red food coloring.

Now look! The reaction between lemon and baking soda will make it look like your lemon is belching.

What is happening here? Lemon contains citric acid, and baking soda is a base. When they mix, a chemical reaction takes place that produces a gas called carbon dioxide. This gas creates bubbles that come out of the lemon, just like an erupting volcano!

Remember, safety first! Make sure you have an adult with you while you do this experiment. And don't forget, chemistry can be fun and spectacular!

Until next time.

4.3 Water and Oil Experiment

Hello, young science explorers! Today we will learn something new and fascinating with a simple experiment that you can do at home. You will need a transparent glass, water, cooking oil and food coloring.

Fill about half of the glass with water.

Add a few drops of food coloring. This step is optional, but it makes the experiment more colorful and fun!

Slowly pour the oil into the glass until it is filled.

See what happens!

You will notice that the oil floats on the water. But why? This happens because oil is less dense than water. Also, water and oil do not mix because water is polar (attracted to other water molecules) and oil is non-polar (not attracted to water molecules).

Always remember that safety is the most important thing! Make sure you have an adult with you during the experiment. And don't forget: science is an adventure, so have fun while you learn!

Until next time.

4.4 Homemade Lava Experiment

Hello, little inventors! Today we will create something really exciting: homemade lava! Yes, you heard me right. Get ready to build your own lava lamp. You will need a transparent glass or jar, cooking oil, water, food coloring and an effervescent tablet (such as Alka-Seltzer).

Fill about 3/4 of the glass with cooking oil.

Add water until the glass is almost full, leaving some space on top.

Add a few drops of food coloring. Choose your favorite color!

Now it's time for magic! Break the effervescent tablet into a couple of pieces and put them in the glass.

Watch as the "lava" starts moving!

What is happening here? The effervescent tablet dissolves in the water creating a gas. This gas rises through the oil creating colored bubbles. These colorful bubbles give the illusion of a lava lamp!

Remember, safety first! Make sure you have an adult with you while you do this experiment. And above all, have fun exploring the wonderful world of chemistry.

Until next time.

4.5 Experiment with the Effervescent Reaction of Lemon and Bicarbonate

Hello, little scientists! Today we will carry out an effervescent experiment with two ingredients that you can easily find at home: lemon and baking soda. You will need a lemon, baking soda, a teaspoon, a glass and, if you want, a little food coloring to add a touch of color.

Cut a lemon in half. This step should be done by an adult.

Squeeze the juice of a lemon into the glass.

Add a teaspoon of baking soda to the glass with the lemon juice.

Observe the reaction! You will see a lot of effervescent bubbles.

What's going on? Lemon juice is acidic, and baking soda is a base. When mixed, they create a chemical reaction that produces a gas called carbon dioxide. This gas is released in the form of bubbles, creating an effervescent effect.

Remember, safety first! Make sure you have an adult with you while you do this experiment. And remember, science is an adventure, so have fun while you learn!

Chapter 5: Experiments on the Nature of Materials

Hello, little explorers! Are you ready to discover the fantastic world of materials? In this chapter, we will show you some interesting experiments that will help you understand how the different materials we see and use every day work. As always, you will need an adult with you. Before starting, ask permission and prepare all the necessary materials together.

Experiment 1: Magnetism

In this experiment, we will find out which materials are attracted to magnets. You will need a magnet and various household items.

Material needed:

1. A strong magnet (like a neodymium magnet)

2. Various household items (for example: pieces of metal, plastic, wood, paper, glass, aluminum, steel, copper, etc.)

3. A clean table or work surface

Procedure:

1. Take your magnet and the objects you have chosen for the experiment and place them on the table.

2. Start with one object at a time. Bring the magnet closer to the object and see if there is any reaction. If the object is attracted towards the magnet, then it is magnetic. If nothing happens, the object is not magnetic.

3. Repeat step 2 for all items you have collected.

4. Once finished, you can create two groups: magnetic and non-magnetic objects.

Explanation:

Magnets attract materials that contain iron, nickel or cobalt. These three elements have special properties that make them magnetic. When a magnetic material is approached to a magnet, the opposite poles of the magnet and the material attract, causing the object to move towards the magnet.

Not all metals are magnetic. For example, aluminum and copper are not attracted to magnets. Similarly, materials such as wood, plastic, glass and paper are not magnetic because they do not contain iron, nickel or cobalt.

This experiment helps you better understand the concept of magnetism and observe which materials in your home are magnetic. Always remember to do scientific experiments in a safe environment and, if possible, under adult supervision. Have fun with science!

Experiment 2: Water absorption

This experiment will show you how different materials absorb water. You will need pieces of different fabrics, a glass of water and a stopwatch.

Material needed:

1. Pieces of different fabrics (cotton, wool, silk, nylon, polyester, etc.)

2. A glass of water

3. A stopwatch

4. A kitchen scale (optional, but useful for a more precise experiment)

Procedure:

1. Take the pieces of fabric and, if you have a scale, weigh each piece before the experiment. Write down the weight of each piece.

2. Fill the glass with water.

3. Completely immerse the first piece of fabric in the water.

4. Start the stopwatch for one minute. During this time, the fabric should absorb water.

5. After one minute, remove the fabric from the water. If you have a scale, weigh the fabric now that it is wet and write down the weight.

6. Repeat steps 3 to 5 for each piece of fabric.

7. Observe and compare how much water each tissue absorbed. If you have used a scale, you can do this by subtracting the initial weight of the fabric from the final weight.

Explanation:

This experiment demonstrates how different materials have different levels of absorbency, i.e. the ability to retain liquids such as water. Some fabrics, such as cotton and wool, are known for their high absorbency. This is due to the fiber structure of these fabrics, which allows water to be retained between the fibers.

Other fabrics, such as nylon and polyester, do not absorb much water. These synthetic fabrics are often hydrophobic, meaning they repel water.

Always remember to do scientific experiments in a safe environment and, if possible, under adult supervision. Have fun with science!

Experiment 3: on Material Flexibility

Hello, young engineers! Today, we will find out how flexible some materials can be. This experiment will help you understand how the different materials we see and use every day work. You will need various materials, such as a pencil, a piece of paper, a piece of plastic, a piece of aluminum and a piece of rubber.

Materials:

A pencil

A piece of paper

A piece of plastic

A piece of aluminum

A piece of rubber

Take one of the materials and try to bend it. Can you fold it easily? Breaks? Does it return to its original form?

Repeat the process for each material and observe the differences.

Record your observations. Which materials are most flexible? Which ones less?

What's going on? Some materials, such as rubber, are very flexible and can be bent easily without breaking. Others, like the pencil, are not flexible and break if you try to bend them. This is a very important property of materials, especially when they are used to build things!

Remember, safety first! Make sure you have an adult with you while you do this experiment. And remember, science is an adventure, so have fun while you learn!

Until next time.

Conclusion

Yes, little explorers, we have come to the end of this fantastic journey through the world of scientific experiments. You've discovered so many new things, haven't you? You have seen how water can behave in surprising ways, how nature operates wonderful processes, how light can play with colors, how chemistry can create spectacular reactions, and how materials can have amazing properties.

Remember, every experiment you have done is a small step toward understanding the world around us. Science is everywhere around us, and with a little curiosity and a little confidence, you can discover incredible things.

I hope these experiments have inspired you to keep exploring, asking questions, and seeking answers. Science is a never-ending adventure, full of discoveries and emotions.

But remember, even if you have finished this book, your journey into science is not over! Keep experimenting, learning and having fun. Always ask an adult for help when doing an experiment and, above all, always respect the safety rules.

Thank you for allowing me to accompany you on this scientific journey. I hope we will meet again in a new adventure! And remember that we are rooting for you little scientists.

Until next time

The FRGG NEW PRESS BOOKS Team

CPSIA information can be obtained
at www.ICGtesting.com
Printed in the USA
BVHW051304130623
665881BV00008B/147

9 781088 139547